The Creation

AN AWESOME BIBLE STORIES ADVENTURE

Edited by John D. Morris

Original text : Albert Hari, Charles Singer
English text : Anne White, Noel Kelly

Illustrations : Mariano Valsesia, Betti Ferrero

CHAPTER · 1

Where Did We Come From?

Michelangelo Buonarroti,
(1475-1564),
The Creation of Adam (detail)

© Alinari-Giraudon / Sistine Chapel, Rome (Vatican)

In the Beginning

Mountains in Southern New Zealand

Mankind has always been fascinated with the subject of origins. But, we are limited to our present time. How can we know what happened before anyone was present to observe actions? Those who have lived in the past could record what they saw, and we can evaluate the accuracy of their writings, but even they were not present to observe long ago origin events.

Science is also limited to the present, as are scientists. Scientists can study what they see and speculate about history, but they can never fully grasp our ultimate origins. Thankfully, in the Bible, God's Word, we have an accurate record of these past events. Here, the Creator Himself told us about the origin of the universe, of the earth, of plants and animals, and of mankind. Because He was there, and told us what He did, we can know. And because He is God, we can trust Him.

Creation is not now occurring, thus we cannot observe the process of creation, only the results of His past supernatural work. Instead, we observe the operation of creation under natural laws He set up. God is resting from creation, but maintaining it through His power.

Creation in Six Days

In the Bible, God tells us what we need to know to understand Him and to understand the creation. He doesn't tell us all the details. He allows us to fill in the details as we study His handiwork, but it does tell us He created all things in six days, not so long ago.

Day One: The heavens and the earth; light

Day Two: The oceans and the atmosphere

Day Three: The continents and plant life

Day Four: The sun, moon and stars

Day Five: Animal life in the ocean and atmosphere

Day Six: Animal life on the continents and mankind

Day Seven: God rested from His completed creation

As we observe the creation, we find that it agrees with God's Record.

Town Clock in Prague, Czech Republic

The Symphony of Creation

Genesis 1 : 1, 3-5, 6, 7c, 8-11, 12c, 13, 14, 16c, 17, 18c, 19, 20, 22-24, 25c, 26a, 27, 28, 31. Genesis 2 : 1, 3.

"In the beginning God created the heaven and the earth."

"And God said, Let there be light : and there was light. And God saw the light, that it was good : and God divided the light from the darkness. And God called the light Day, and the darkness he called Night. And the evening and the morning were the first day."

"And God said, Let there be a firmament in the midst of the waters, . . . And God made the firmament, and divided the waters which were under the firmament from the waters which were above the firmament : and it was so. And God called the firmament Heaven. And the evening and the morning were the second day."

"And God said, Let the waters under the heaven be gathered together unto one place, and let the dry land appear ; and it was so. And God called the dry land Earth ; and the gathering together of the waters called he Seas ; and God saw that it was good. And God said, Let the earth bring forth grass, the herb yielding seed, and the fruit tree yielding fruit after his kind, whose seed is in itself, upon the earth : and it was so. And God saw that it was good. And the evening and the morning were the third day."

"And God said, Let there be lights in the firmament of the heaven to divide the day from the night ; and let them be for signs, and for seasons, and for days, and years : " . . .

"And God made two great lights ; the greater light to rule the day, and the lesser light to rule the night : He made the stars also . . . to divide the light from the darkness : and God saw that it was good. And the evening and the morning were the fourth day."

"And God said, Let the waters bring forth abundantly the moving creature that hath life, and fowl that may fly above the earth in the open firmament of heaven." and God saw that it was good. "And God blessed them, saying, Be fruitful and multiply, and fill the waters in the seas, and let fowl multiply in the earth. And the evening and the morning were the fifth day."

"And God said, Let the earth bring forth the living creature after his kind, cattle, and creeping thing, and beast of the earth after his kind : and it was so. And God saw that it was good. And God said, Let us make man in our image, after our likeness : So God created man in his own image, in the image of God created he him ; male and female created he them. And God blessed them, and God said unto them, Be fruitful, and multiply, and replenish the earth, and subdue it : and have dominion over the fish of the sea, and over the fowl of the air, and over every living thing that moveth upon the earth. And God saw every thing that he had made, and, behold, it was very good. And the evening and the morning were the sixth day."

"Thus the heavens and the earth were finished, and all the host of them." "And God blessed the seventh day, and sanctified it : because that in it he had rested from all his work which God created and made."

Mankind

There are certain similarities between man and the animals. After all, we live in the same environment and depend on the same food, water and air. But the differences, such as brain size, are great. Man did not descend from the animals.

Creation

God is a God of order. His creation was in an orderly progression, preparing the earth for man. First there was light, air, water, land, plants, sunlight, fish, birds, animals.

In God's Image

Mankind adequately reflects God's Image, not in his bodily form, but in his spiritual nature. Appreciation for beauty, knowledge of right and wrong, desire to love and be loved, ability to communicate etc. These are godly characteristics which He imparts only to mankind. God values each human being, and so should we.

The Creation

The Source of Life

There is a law in science that life comes only from life. The original life came from the living God. Death was not a part of His original creation.

Very Good

God created everything perfect, exactly as He wanted and consistent with His character. He crowned His creation with His image in mankind. Man was in perfect fellowship with God and in harmony with each other and with creation.

Loving

Love characterizes our Creator. If we are to reflect His image properly we would love as He loves – in a selfless, sacrificial way – recognizing the great worth of our neighbor.

Choices

Our greatest desire, as possessors of the *"image of God"*, should be to please Him in all that we do. Scripture reveals Him as totally without fault, and while none of us are able to live up to His absolute standard, this must be our goal. He commands, "Be ye holy, for I am holy" (I Peter 1:16).

Abilities

God has granted us the privilege of sharing in His work. We can communicate, think, serve, organize, and make new things out of what He has created. We can decide correctly, using His value system. We can be His instruments, extending His love to those around us.

You are Able!

"Be creators!" says God.

"Be creators, like me!
Be inventors! You can!"

What incredible news!
What a fantastic plan!

God calls everyone.
Each person must be
a creator with
the wonders we see:

creator of goodness
inventor of sharing
sculptor of beauty
crafter of peace
designer of kindness
sower of comfort
seeker after friendship
explorer of hope
giver of love.

God-gifted, each person
is part of the making,
creating and shaping
the Creator began.

CHAPTER 2

The Beautiful Garden

A modern stained glass window, Louis Apffel Street, Strasbourg, France

© F. Zvardon

Life in a "Very Good" World

Farmer working in his field

Can you imagine what life would be like in a perfect world? It would be very different from the life we know. There would be no hunger, no sickness, no pain, no fear of animals, no unkind words, certainly no war. Water would flow freely, flowers would bloom without thorns, and abundant crops would gladden the heart. Best of all, creation would be in perfect fellowship with the Creator. There would be no rebellion against His wishes, no wrong choices.

Such was the case in the beginning, as man was placed in the beautiful Garden of Eden. Every need was supplied, especially direct access to God and His wisdom. They had access to the majestic Tree of Life, through which they would live forever in constant health.

Blessing Comes with Responsibility

A perfect life would not be a life free of duties. The Creator wisely gave Adam and Eve tasks to accomplish, through which they would gain the satisfaction of a job well done, and of pleasing their gracious Creator. They were given stewardship over the Garden, to maintain its order and beauty, and to study their environment and apply what they learned for man's good, and God's glory. They were given dominion over the animals, not in a harsh sense, but to care for them as God had cared for them. Their very bodies were also endowed with the privilege of, through their union, creating other eternal souls, each with the ability to love God.

They were also given an opportunity to prove their love for God. In the Garden was another tree, the Tree of the Knowledge of Good and Evil. They were warned not to eat of it, for if they did, the fellowship with God would be broken. God's nature of absolute holiness would demand that any who chose disobedience must be driven from His presence and from the Tree of Life. Both spiritually and physically "the wages of sin is death" (Romans 67 : 23).

Woman slicing pineapple in Guatemala

Food for the Animals
There was to be no carnivorous activity in the original "very good" earth. Both man and the animals were to eat plants only (Gen 1 : 29,30). All living things, (defined in the Bible as having the "breath of life" and "blood" in their veins) were to be herbivorous. Plants are biologically alive, but not "alive" in the Biblical use of the term.

B i b l e

The Story of the Creation

Genesis 2 : 4, 7-9, 10a, 15-18, 20-24.

"These are the generations of the heavens and of the earth when they were created, in the day that the LORD God made the earth and the heavens...

And the LORD God formed man of the dust of the ground, and breathed into his nostrils the breath of life; and man became a living soul. And the LORD God planted a garden eastward in Eden ; and there he put the man whom he had formed. And out of the ground made the LORD God to grow every tree that is pleasant to the sight, and good for food : the Tree of Life also in the midst of the garden, and the Tree of Knowledge of Good and Evil. And a river went out of Eden to water the garden;"

"And the LORD God took the man, and put him into the garden of Eden to dress it and to keep it. And the LORD God commanded the man, saying, Of every tree of the garden thou mayest freely eat. But of the Tree of the Knowledge of Good and Evil, thou shalt not eat of it: for in the day that thou eatest thereof thou shalt surely die.

And the LORD God said, It is not good that the man should be alone; I will make him an help meet for him."...

"And Adam gave names to all cattle, and to the foul of the air, and to every beast of the field ; but for Adam there was not found an help meet for him. And the LORD God caused a deep sleep to fall upon Adam and he slept : and he took one of his ribs, and closed up the flesh instead thereof ; And the rib, which the LORD God had taken from man, made he a woman, and brought her unto the man. And Adam said, This is now bone of my bones, and flesh of my flesh : she shall be called Woman, because she was taken out of Man. Therefore shall a man leave his father and his mother, and shall cleave unto his wife : and they shall be one flesh."

One Flesh

When Jesus defended the sanctity of marriage, He explained that the one man/one woman lifelong relationship was the Creator's "very good" plan for mankind.

Eden

Although Eden was a special garden, the entire earth was perfect. Adam was given the two-fold responsibility of filling the earth with his descendants, and extending Eden's blessings to all corners of the globe.

Two trees

The Tree of Life may have been a special blessing but it was not an eternal fountain of youth, nor did the Tree of Knowledge of Good and Evil contain a poison. Rather it is obedience to God which brings life and disobedience which brings death.

In God's Image

Equals

Men and women have been given different strengths and functions, but they are of equal worth in God's eyes. If we would please him, we would have the same attitude.

Men

While much variety exists, men tend to be more concerned with protecting and providing for their families. God has given them leadership roles in family and church, but also greater responsibility.

Women

Within the obvious variety, women tend to be more involved in the nurturing and caring roles in the family. They are to work together toward the same goals. She is to help the man fulfill his God-given role.

A Perfect Combination

God's Image consists of both man and woman. It takes the abilities, strengths, and personalities of both, working in unified harmony, to adequately reflect God's Image.

Marriage

Just as Eve was taken from Adam's side, thus they were truly "one flesh", a man and woman can become "one flesh" in a God-honoring marriage relationship.

Signs of God

They are there on earth
and in the vastness of the
universe
signs of God too many to be
counted,
signs of the Creator of life.

All we need do is
lift up our eyes
to the stars scattered over the blanket
of heaven,
taste the wind
and the smell of spring
feel water
swirling over rounded pebbles,
watch penguins
in their party clothes.

That's all it takes to be filled with wonder
in the presence of God
at whose word life pours forth

All we need do is
look with wonder
at the beauty of love between
woman and man
make time to enjoy
the smiles of children
stand amazed
at how people care for
one another
forgetful of self.

That's all it takes to be filled
with wonder
in the presence of God
in whose image we're
made.

CHAPTER 3

Paradise Lost

You will have to sweat to earn a living.
This Picture by anonymous is an illustration of the consequences of separation between humanity and God The Creator. The desire to break away from God's presence will also bring separation between man and woman, humanity and nature. In the background of this picture, the high walls of the city hide its isolated inhabitants and the faces of the workers express anxiety, hardship, sadness and solitude.

© F. Zardon

Why Have Things Changed?

A serpent

Life in God's special garden was paradise on earth, with every need provided in ample supply. Tasks and responsibilities brought only pleasure. But now paradise has faded from view. Life today has difficulties – from natural catastrophes to disease, to famine, to broken relationships, to consequences of wrong choices, either our wrong choices or those of others.

Adam and Eve made a wrong choice, with disastrous consequences. They chose to directly disobey God's one commandment which carried a penalty. Until then they knew only "good", but under the temptation of Satan they chose to eat of the Tree of the Knowledge of Good **and** Evil! And from then on they and all their descendants knew evil.

Farmer tilling his land

Satan's Tools of Deception

Satan could not have been present on earth in its "very good" state or else it would not have been very good. He had been banished to earth for his heavenly rebellion against God. In a rage, he sought to ruin creation and mock God by breaking the sweet fellowship between God and His newly created image.

First he placed the seed of doubt in Eve's mind. Is God really good when He has denied you this fruit? With the wedge driven in, he convinced her there are no consequences to sin. Then he appealed to her fleshly appetite, her desire to take whatever she saw and her prideful thirst for hidden wisdom. She wanted to be as a god herself. Thus she chose to flaunt her freedom and reject her loving Creator's one rule. She chose to disobey and Adam willingly followed. But disobedience is sin, and sin brings consequences.

How Long?
The Bible doesn't say how much time elapsed between Creation and Adam's sin, but it doesn't appear to have been very long. Adam and Eve had been commanded to "be fruitful and multiply". They were fully obedient and fully healthy, yet they had not conceived.

Sin and its Consequences

Genesis 3 : 1-20.

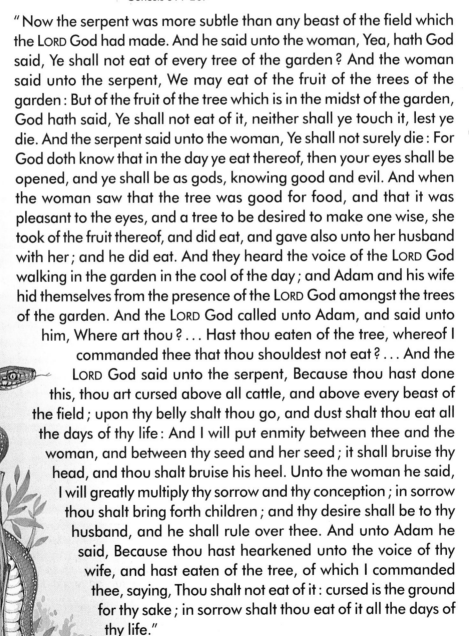

" Now the serpent was more subtle than any beast of the field which the LORD God had made. And he said unto the woman, Yea, hath God said, Ye shall not eat of every tree of the garden ? And the woman said unto the serpent, We may eat of the fruit of the trees of the garden : But of the fruit of the tree which is in the midst of the garden, God hath said, Ye shall not eat of it, neither shall ye touch it, lest ye die. And the serpent said unto the woman, Ye shall not surely die : For God doth know that in the day ye eat thereof, then your eyes shall be opened, and ye shall be as gods, knowing good and evil. And when the woman saw that the tree was good for food, and that it was pleasant to the eyes, and a tree to be desired to make one wise, she took of the fruit thereof, and did eat, and gave also unto her husband with her ; and he did eat. And they heard the voice of the LORD God walking in the garden in the cool of the day ; and Adam and his wife hid themselves from the presence of the LORD God amongst the trees of the garden. And the LORD God called unto Adam, and said unto him, Where art thou ? . . . Hast thou eaten of the tree, whereof I commanded thee that thou shouldest not eat ? . . . And the LORD God said unto the serpent, Because thou hast done this, thou art cursed above all cattle, and above every beast of the field ; upon thy belly shalt thou go, and dust shalt thou eat all the days of thy life : And I will put enmity between thee and the woman, and between thy seed and her seed ; it shall bruise thy head, and thou shalt bruise his heel. Unto the woman he said, I will greatly multiply thy sorrow and thy conception ; in sorrow thou shalt bring forth children ; and thy desire shall be to thy husband, and he shall rule over thee. And unto Adam he said, Because thou hast hearkened unto the voice of thy wife, and hast eaten of the tree, of which I commanded thee, saying, Thou shalt not eat of it : cursed is the ground for thy sake ; in sorrow shalt thou eat of it all the days of thy life."

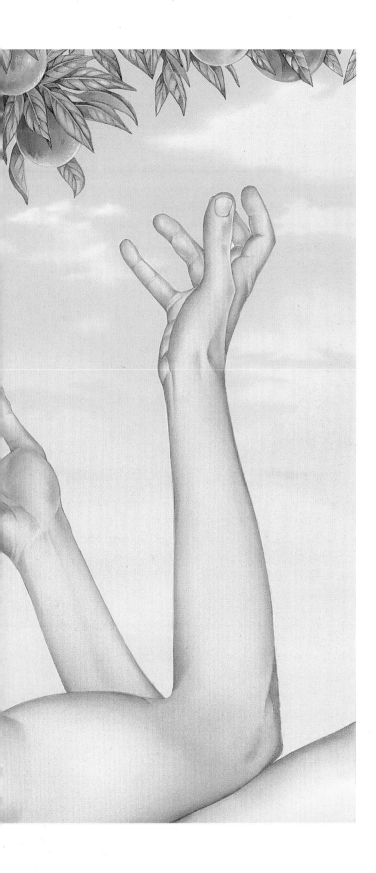

The Animal Kingdom

The Serpent, the animal employed by Satan to tempt Eve, was cursed to a greater extent than "all cattle and above every beast". Thus all the animal kingdom suffered the consequences of Adam's rebellion.

The Plant Kingdom

Even the plant's perfect status was lost. From then on they would bring forth "thorns and thistles", and crops would result only from diligent and sorrowful toil. Even the very earth was cursed.

Human Kind

Adam and Eve bore the brunt of the consequences. Their relationship with God was broken, and their relationship to one another would be stressed. Childbirth would be sorrowful. They, who would have lived forever, would ultimately die. Sin had ruined God's "very good" creation.

Why is there Evil ?

A Universal Law

Looking around, we see that "the whole creation groaneth and travaileth in pain" (Romans 8 : 22) under the effects of sin and the curse. Now everything is trapped in a spiral of death and decay. The sun burns out. The moon's orbit decays. Machines wear out. Our bodies get sick and die.

Adam's Willful Choice

Eve was deceived and chose to rebel, but Adam made a knowledgeable choice. (I Timothy 2 : 14). God cursed the creation, not for Eve's action, but for Adam's willful rejection.

We Would Do The Same

How often do we purposely sin ? How often do we reject our Creator's clear commands and do that which we know we shouldn't ? Do we ever feel that we are missing something good ? We have God's entire Word – we know better – but still we often choose wrong.

Things Haven't Changed

Satan's methods of temptation haven't changed. He still uses the same tricks he used on Eve. He tempts us to doubt God's Word, then he dangles "the lust of the flesh, the lust of the eyes and the pride of life" (I John 2 : 16) before us.

A Way of Escape

Thankfully, we have the power to choose right. "There has no temptation taken you, but such as is common to man : but God is faithful, who will not suffer you to be tempted above that ye are able; but will with the temptation also make a way of escape." (I Cor. 10 : 13).

Don't Give In!

Evil takes advantage
of human weakness,
and worms its way
into the hearts of men and women...
children too!

If they try to ignore evil,
it gets a grip on them
like a parasite.

If they open the door
of their hearts to evil,
then it sets up its kingdom in them

Evil, which they've allowed to find a home
within them,
affects their words, their deeds and their
plans,
making them spiteful
horrible and poisonous.

But human persons are able
to resist the evil
which tries to deface
the image and likeness of God within
them.
And God within helps them
to say "no" to evil
and "yes" to good.

Brothers at War

Iacopo Negretti,
(1480-1528), Cain kills Abel

© AKG Paris - Kunsthistorisches Museum, Wien (Austria)

Life After the Curse

Nomads in the Syrian desert

Even though the world in the days following Adam suffered under the penalty for sin, it was still a wonderful world. People lived to great ages. Families were large. Remnants we can see today of that world shows us that the land was fertile and water was abundant. People had every reason to acknowledge God's goodness and come to worship Him as He desired.

God had given instruction for proper worship. His holiness demands that sin's penalty of death be paid. Worshipers must repent of their sin and offer a blood sacrifice for atonement. A lamb's blood could not fully atone of course, but it was a visual reminder of sin's seriousness, and an act of faith in God's final solution.

Adam and Eve seem to have repented for their sin, for the names they chose for their children remembered God's promise that "the seed of the woman" would ultimately break the serpent's power.

Cain and Abel

Adam and Eve's first two sons were very different. Abel was "righteous" (Matthew 23:35) but Cain was "of that wicked one" (I John 3:12). When it came time to make sacrifice, Abel obeyed God's commands to bring a blood sacrifice, but Cain chose to deny the consequences of his sin, and brought only fruit and grain to the sacrifice. God accepted Abel's obedience, and rejected Cain's disobedience. Cain's prideful nature drove him to kill his brother. Sin's seduction had come to its fullest expression. His pride and self-righteousness even caused him to deny his act when confronted by the all-seeing God. "Am I my brother's keeper?" he retorted. But, as always, sin has its consequences, and Cain's penalty was severe. What would have happened if he had confessed his sin to God and fully repented? He could have gained the sweet restoration of God's forgiveness, but he chose otherwise.

Shepherd in the French Alps

Why Blood Sacrifices?
In God's holy economy, "the wages of sin is death" (Romans 6:23). Sinful man must either pay his own penalty or an adequate substitute must be found - a sinless substitute which has no death penalty on his head. An animal sacrifice only looks forward to the final and completely sufficient sacrifice of the God/man, Jesus Christ, for our sins.

21

Am I My Brother's Keeper?

Genesis 4 : 1-16.

"And Adam knew Eve his wife; and she conceived, and bare Cain, and said, I have gotten a man from the LORD. And she again bare his brother Abel. And Abel was a keeper of sheep, but Cain was a tiller of the ground.

And in process of time it came to pass, that Cain brought of the fruit of the ground an offering unto the LORD. And Abel, he also brought of the firstlings of his flock and of the fat thereof. And the LORD had respect unto Abel and to his offering: But unto Cain and to his offering He had not respect.

And Cain was very wroth, and his countenance fell. And the LORD said unto Cain, Why art thou wroth? and why is thy countenance fallen? If thou doest well, shalt thou not be accepted? and if thou doest not well, sin lieth at the door. And unto thee shall be his desire, and thou shalt rule over him.

And Cain talked with Abel his brother: and it came to pass, when they were in the field, that Cain rose up against Abel his brother, and slew him. And the LORD said unto Cain, Where is Abel thy brother? And He said, I know not: Am I my brother's keeper? And he said, What hast thou done? the voice of thy brother's blood crieth unto me from the ground. And now art thou cursed from the earth, which hath opened her mouth to receive thy brother's blood from thy hand; When thou tillest the ground, it shall not henceforth yield unto thee her strength; a fugitive and a vagabond shalt thou be in the earth. And Cain said unto the LORD, My punishment is greater than I can bear. And Cain went out from the presence of the LORD, and dwelt in the land of Nod, on the east of Eden."

Fugitive

By the time Cain and Abel were adults, there may have been a sizeable population. The Bible says Adam and Eve had other sons and daughters, maybe many more (Genesis 5:4). In the early days, so soon after Adam's creation in perfection with no genetic defects, there would have been no harm in marrying a close relative. Cain must have married a sister or a niece and started a new civilization in the land of Nod.

Civilization

The early human race was not primitive in any sense. The Bible indicates (Genesis 5:17-16) that they built cities, employed ranching and farming, used wind and string musical instruments, and worked metal. Unfortunately they soon were also very wicked.

The Remnant

While Cain and his descendants fully renounced God's ways, Adam's son Seth fathered a line of which some (including Enos, Enoch and Noah) chose to worship God.

Rich Differences

Hatred

Many today are consumed by hatred. Often we hate that which we don't fully understand or that which is different from us. Is it pride which claims "I am better than him ," or a selfish desire to have what he has ? When we yield to such feelings, are we different than Cain ?

Blood

Throughout history mankind's hatred, lust and pride have erupted into war. No year of recent times has been without war somewhere on earth. In fact, wars seem to be increasing.

All Are Brothers

All people on earth are descended from Adam. From Adam we have inherited the remainder of the "Image of God". Each individual is of great worth to God and all are brothers, in the extended human family. Our world desperately needs to be reminded of this.

All Are Sinners

From Adam we all have also inherited a sin nature. All of us choose wrong, and reject our Creator's guidelines for life and worship, and deserve sin's death penalty. All of us need a savior.

My Brother's Keeper

We can choose to treat our brothers and sisters in righteousness, affording them the dignity and worth due the image of God. We are also privileged to point them to the final payment for sin, the substitutional sacrifice of God's Son, Jesus Christ, for our sins.

Do You Know Your Brothers and Sisters?

Have you thought what being human means?
Surely it's being part of the great human family
which takes its life from God?
Surely it's responding to God's call to live in the love planted in us?

Have you thought about what being a family means?
Does everyone try to love their own brother, sister,
parents and relations with all their strength?
Does each member of the family try to look out for the others
and do whatever would make them most happy?

Deep in the heart of every human person God asks:
"What are you doing about your brothers and sisters?
Are you bothered about them?
Do you try to lighten their burden?
What are you doing to fight hatred and violence?
What are you doing to help people in trouble?
What are you doing to help people live in peace?
What are you doing so
that people can
restore fellowship
with their Creator?

Two Judgements

Snellinck Jan (17th century),
Copy after a picture
of Jan I Brueghel, (1568-1625),
Noah's Ark

© Giraudon - Sforzesco Castle, Miland (Italy)

The Flood of Noah's Day

A mountain stream in Norway

Sin and wickedness increased worldwide in the generations following Adam. Violence was everywhere among both man and the animals, inspired by Satanic influence and involvement. Evil reigned until God intervened. His judgement halted this full-scale rebellion against God and His principles. God's nature has never changed. Sin's penalty has always been death. In Noah's day, this punishment took the form of a world-wide flood.

A righteous remnant remained throughout this rebellion, but soon all had either fallen away or been martyred, all except Noah. In obedience to God, he built a huge boat, large enough to carry his family and two of each kind of land-dwelling, air-breathing animal, to preserve them from the water cataclysm. Noah's faith and obedience are examples to all who follow.

Confusion at the Tower of Babel

As Noah and the animals left the ark following the flood, God commanded them to multiply and fill the earth with their descendants. The animals obeyed. Polar ice caps grew large after the flood, trapping huge volumes of water on the continents. This lowered sea levels by about 600 feet, and all the continents were connected by land or ice bridges.

However, mankind still refused to obey, and built a monument to keep them all together – a tower from which they could worship the stars of heaven, rejecting the Creator of heaven and earth. But God's purposes will be accomplished. He confused their languages, bringing the construction project to a halt, forcing the individual language groups away from one another to live in peace. Within just a few generations every corner of the globe was inhabited, just as God intended.

Building the Tower of Babel, taken from a 15th Century miniature

Was There Enough Water?
If the high mountains and the deep oceans were leveled off to a completely smooth sphere, the waters would cover the earth to a depth of about 10,000 feet. There's plenty of water to cover the earth.

The Table of Nations
Genesis 10 gives us a list of 70 different language groups and their migratory destinations. Scientists have found this an amazingly accurate document.

The Rainbow

Genesis 6:1-22 ; 7:11-12 ; 8:18-19 ; 9:1 ; 10:1, 32, 11:1-9.

" And it came to pass, when men began to multiply on the face of the earth, and daughters were born unto them, That the sons of God saw the daughters of men that they were fair ; and they took them wives of all which they chose … And God saw that the wickedness of man was great in the earth, and that every imagination of the thoughts of his heart was only evil continually. And it repented the LORD that He had made man on the earth, and it grieved Him at his heart. And the LORD said, I will destroy man whom I have created from the face of the earth ; both man, and beast, and the creeping thing, and the fowls of the air ; for it repenteth me that I have made them. But Noah found grace in the eyes of the LORD … And God said unto Noah, The end of all flesh is come before me ; for the earth is filled with violence through them ; and, behold, I will destroy them with the earth. Make thee an ark of gopher wood ; … And, behold, I, even I, do bring a flood of waters upon the earth to destroy all flesh, wherein is the breath of life, from under heaven ; and every thing that is in the earth shall die.

But with thee will I establish my covenant ; and thou shalt come into the ark, thou, and thy sons, and thy wife, and thy sons' wives with thee. And of every living thing of all flesh, two of every sort shalt thou bring into the ark, to keep them alive with thee ; they shall be male and female …Thus did Noah ; according to all that God commanded him, so did he."

"In the six hundredth year of Noah's life, in the second month, the seventeenth day of the month, the same day were all the fountains of the great deep broken up, and the windows of heaven were opened. And the rain was upon the earth forty days and forty nights …"

"And Noah went forth, and his sons, and his wife, and his sons' wives with him : Every beast, every creeping thing, and every fowl, and whatsoever creepeth upon the earth, after their kinds, went forth out of the ark … And God blessed Noah and his sons, and said unto them, Be fruitful, and multiply, and replenish the earth.

Now these are the generations of the sons of Noah, Shem, Ham, and Japheth : and unto them were sons born after the Flood … These are the families of the sons of Noah, after their generations, in their nations : and by these were the nations divided in the earth after the Flood.

And the whole earth was of one language, and of one speech.

And they said, Go to, let us build us a city and a tower, whose top may reach unto heaven ; and let us make us a name, lest we be scattered abroad upon the face of the whole earth … And the LORD said, Behold, the people is one, and they have all one language ; and this they begin to do : and now nothing will be restrained from them, which they have imagined to do. Go to, let us go down, and there confound their language, that they may not understand one another's speech. So the LORD scattered them abroad from thence upon the face of all the earth: and they left off to build the city.

Language

Seldom do countries live at peace when they don't speak the same language. Communication is necessary for understanding. In separating the languages, God forced migration to occur. The resulting national units expose mankind's sinful tendencies and his desperate need for a Savior.

The Tower

Ziggurats, or pyramid shaped towers, have been found around the world. Each was built to worship the sun or stars, in direct rebellion against God. The peoples migrating from Babel took the tower's design and purpose with them, continuing their long, Satanically energized, war against God.

Sons of God

This term is used only for beings directly created by God. The difficult passage in Genesis 6 suggests demonic (i.e. fallen angels) involvement in the rebellion against God before the Flood. The sinful episode warranted God's judgement, but even in judgement God is gracious. His rainbow covenant with man promised no such watery destruction would ever occur again.

The rainbow of God

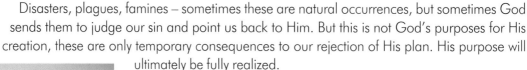

Misfortunes

Disasters, plagues, famines – sometimes these are natural occurrences, but sometimes God sends them to judge our sin and point us back to Him. But this is not God's purposes for His creation, these are only temporary consequences to our rejection of His plan. His purpose will ultimately be fully realized.

Diversity

Just as migrating animals adapted to new conditions and new environments after the flood – some acquiring novel characteristics and others a taste for meat – so migrating human language groups acquired new features. The varied skin colors are adaptations from the brown-skin of Noah's family. Skin color shouldn't separate such close relatives.

Bridges

If we would please our Creator, we would do our best to heal past wounds. God is pleased when peace prevails. We should be instruments of peace, taking God's message of love and forgiveness to all.

A Great Gulf

Man's sin is the chief culprit. It has separated us from our God. He is loving and forgiving, yes, but He is also holy and cannot allow sinners into His presence. Man can do nothing on his own to restore this broken relationship with God.

The Final Solution

Sin's penalty, death, must be paid. God's holiness and justice demands it. Since man is powerless to escape God's punishment, God has paid the penalty Himself. The death of Christ on the cross substituted for the death we deserve. His resurrection from the dead sealed the victory. This is our only hope, our urgent message to the nations.

Babel

Babel,
It's the chaos that happens
when people refuse to listen
to each other,
when they eye each other
spitefully,
like enemies spitting hate and
saying:
We're more important than you.

Babel
It's when pride takes hold
and people think they are all powerful.
That they are a match for God.

Babel comes to an end
when harmony reigns on earth,
when people build bridges
across what divides them,
when they start to talk to each other
and build peace...

Babel comes to an end
when human beings
pool their efforts to look after the
creation
turn to God and ask:
Help us, Lord to accept the
restored
fellowship which you offer
Help us share with clarity
the message of your
sacrificial love.

Man's Position in Creation

As God's crowning achievement, as the very image of God, man has a position of leadership over creation. He was told to "subdue" creation, and was given "dominion" over the earth and all the animals.

Proper Stewardship

Some have misapplied this principle and justified exploiting the environment, doing lasting harm. But this cannot be supported from Scripture. The followers of God should understand this as a command to care for the environment, and use it wisely for man's good and God's glory.

Use of Science and Technology

The best interpretation of "subdue" is to *study* the creation, and *understand* it fully. This is the function of "science", like biology, geology, physics, meteorology, etc. Once the knowledge is gained it must be properly *applied* to exercise "dominion". This is the realm of "technology", like medicine, mining, engineering, weather modifications, etc..

Environmentalism

The modern day environmental movement contains many illegitimate aspects. To consider that "man is the enemy" – that animal rights supersede human rights, that trees have feelings – cannot be supported by science, Scripture or plain sense. The creation must not be worshipped, as the modern New Age Movement contends, but, protecting and properly utilizing the environment is the Christian's duty.

In the Beginning

The original earth was in perfect balance. No pollutants, no natural disasters, no lack of water or fertile soil. Adam and Eve's sinful choice brought consequences which impacted even the environment. The pre-flood world, while retaining much of creation's original perfection, was forever altered by the great flood of Noah's day. The world today, severely out of balance, and abused by human greed and neglect, demands our immediate attention.

Paradise Restored

God's intention for creation, rejected from the start, will ultimately come to fruition. For those who have accepted His free gift of forgiveness and eternal life, based on the sacrificial death and victorious resurrection of Jesus Christ, heaven awaits. Heaven includes full fellowship with our Creator, restored access to the Tree of Life, fulfilling duties and responsibilities, which will never end.

The Good News

"The wages of sin is death, but the gift of God is eternal life through Jesus Christ our Lord" (Romans 6:23), for "Christ died for our sins" (I Corinthians 15:3). This truth must be believed and accepted. "By grace are we saved through faith, and not of works, lest any man should boast" (Ephesians 2:8-9). This is good news indeed!

What God Expects Of Us

Once our relationship with God is restored, we have certain duties to perform. One is to carry out our responsibility of stewardship over creation, wisely caring for our dominion. Two, in our every action, whether we "eat, or drink, or whatsoever ye do, do all to the glory of God" (I Corinthians 10:31). Three, we are to be "ambassadors for Christ, . . . we pray you in Christ's stead, be ye reconciled to God" (I Corinthians 5:20), through faith in the finished work of His Son, our Lord and Savior Jesus Christ.

A F i n a l N o t e :

The beauty and majesty of God's creation is enjoyed by everyone. Every time we take a breath or splash cool water on our faces, our Creator is reminding us that He is with us, and was there in the beginning to make our world.

That first world was perfect, but sin ruined everything. People began to die, and animals became violent. It became necessary for God to send a Redeemer to us.

Now, the only way we can know these things is to read it in Genesis. That was God's way of helping us know where we came from, and more importantly, where we're going. All of us wonder about our surroundings. We want to know who we are.

Wonderfully, God has given us a true account of creation, so that we will see how much He loves us. People are made in God's image, which means we can think, love, hope, and accomplish things. They try to prove that there is no God. But the Creator has told us all His words are true, giving us a peace that lasts forever.